Ga...
FOR THE
NHS

Gags
FOR THE
NHS

PHIL EVANS AND DILWYN PHILLIPS

First impression: 2020
© Phil Evans, Dilwyn Phillips & Y Lolfa Cyf., 2020

Cover design: Y Lolfa
Cartoons: Freda Ayers and Morgan Tomos

ISBN: 978 1 78461 941 1

Published and printed in Wales
on paper from well-maintained forests by
Y Lolfa Cyf., Talybont, Ceredigion SY24 5HE
e-mail ylolfa@ylolfa.com
website www.ylolfa.com
tel 01970 832 304
fax 832 782

Introduction

During the pandemic, our dedicated, hard-working front-line workers in all professions have proved that a healthy sense of humour is vital to help them cope with the enormous pressure they're under, acting as an invisible shield against any possibility of their being completely overwhelmed by the enormity of their daily tasks.

And for the rest of us, humour promotes wellbeing by allowing us to step back and take a slightly different look at life's stressful situations and painful emotions, without diminishing their importance or the effect they can have on us and the people we care about.

You could say that humour is the glue that binds us all together.

Laughter reduces stress, boosts your immune system, helps reduce blood pressure and exercises your diaphragm, stomach, chest, neck and other muscles. It should be manufactured in tablet form and made available on the National Health so you could take one every morning after breakfast.

Laughing a hundred times a day is the

equivalent of fifteen minutes on an exercise bike or ten minutes on a rowing machine. Ken Dodd knew what he was talking about when he told his audience he'd soon have them exercising their 'chuckle muscles'!

Dilwyn Phillips and I do hope that you enjoy our creative collaboration and that the humour within provides some much-needed escapism and brings a smile to your face every time you dip into it.

We truly appreciate being given the opportunity to write this book for which all profits in the UK will be donated to NHS charities and books sold in Spain to Spanish hospitals.

Our thanks to Y Lolfa for their help, guidance and support in getting it into print.

Bless you all,
Phil Evans

Jokes by Phil Evans

Lockdown

Over the Covid-19 lockdown I discovered a few things about myself and the world we now live in. Let me explain …

My car is capable of doing six weeks to the gallon.

The money I saved on petrol had gone towards gym membership and I started going twice a day. It was closed, but the walk there and back did me good.

I also discovered that you should never tell your other half that you can see her grey roots when she's halfway through cutting your hair with electric hair clippers. I had to wear a bobble hat as well as a mask and gloves. Previously, if I'd have walked into the bank looking like this, they'd have activated the alarm.

Covid-19 has changed me. I had a call asking me if I'd had an accident in the last three years and I kept the young man on the phone for over two hours just for a chat. Well, I never thought

I'd say this, but I do miss the Brexit debates now.

Right then. I must dash. I'm off to buy a bucket – it's at the top of my list.

If I was Prime Minister

I would improve the NHS by turning all their offices into wards and all their pen-pushers into nurses. And make them wear badges that display their annual salary.

★

I would solve the problem of bed-blocking by installing all hospital beds with ejector seats that activate after three days.

★

I would reduce NHS waiting lists by cancelling the appointments of anyone with a double-barrelled surname. And anyone called Sinjen.

★

I would punish all terrorists by making them live outdoors in the Orkney Islands in the middle of winter. Naked.

★

I would ban 24-hour news channels and replace them with repeats of *Friends*.

★

I would replace advertising billboards with positive messages such as "Everything is going to be okay".

★

I would force people to believe that "I Can't Believe It's Not Butter" is not butter. Why? Because there's too much cynicism in this country and it needs stamping out.

★

I would put electro-shock machines into the seats at the Houses of Parliament that would give MPs and Lords a sharp buzz every ten minutes to stop them falling asleep.

★

I would make MPs wear the logos of all the companies they have a financial interest in on their clothes.

★

I would make every Monday a Bank Holiday Monday, thereby creating the three-day weekend. And free ice-creams for all.

★

I would crush the car of every motorist caught using their mobile phone while driving. And the guilty drivers would have to watch them being crushed. Then they would be given a child's tricycle to use instead.

★

I would ban all music made after the year 2000 and make primary school children take mandatory lessons in The Beatles and Elvis Presley. There would be repeats of Top Of The Pops running all day, every day, on its own terrestrial TV channel.

★

I would make the supermarkets get rid of all self-service checkouts and replace them with TWO human cashiers. On £20 an hour each. And replace the board of directors at each of those supermarkets with robots. See how they like it!

★

I'd build an army of drones to look out for dog owners who don't clean up after their pets. Every time a drone spotted somebody not picking up dog poo, the drone would do it for them and then drop it on their head.

★

I would force the Queen to live in a tower block on a council estate, and turn Buckingham Palace into accommodation for thousands of students. Central London would become the party capital of the world.

★

I would make parking free for all. Although, that would mean parking would become a free-for-all. It'd be chaos.

★

I'd pump Prozac into the drinking water and marijuana into the air-conditioning system. Because a happy, chilled out nation is a productive nation. Plus shares in chocolate biscuits would skyrocket.

★

I'd merge public libraries with public houses. If everyone tries to put the world to rights over a pint of beer, it'd be a good idea if they were better informed beforehand.

★

I'd ban all call centres, and make everyone of their employees visit their customer's homes to sort out their problem over a nice cup of tea.

Things I've learned

Never take a sleeping pill and a laxative on the same night...

★

It's a fact of life that everyone has an annoying friend. If you don't have one, it's probably you.

★

Want people to pay attention to you? Try saying, "I shouldn't be telling you this", at the beginning of every conversation.

★

If you're going to be a smart-ass, first make sure you're smart. Otherwise you're just an ass.

★

You know that "little thing" inside your head that keeps you from saying things you shouldn't? I don't have one of those.

★

I shouldn't be telling you this.

★

A quiet man is a thinking man. A quiet woman is usually mad.

★

Ever notice that when you get tired, everyone else gets stupid?

Take some advice
Have you had a hard week in work? You should have worked harder in school then, shouldn't you?

★

Isn't it strange that drivers that go slower than you are idiots… and those that go faster than you are maniacs?

★

Why is common sense so rare these days?

★

Life isn't like a bowl of cherries – it's more like a hot curry. What you do today, might burn you tomorrow.

★

He was once described as being multi-talented... which meant that he could talk and annoy you at the same time.

★

When your back is against the wall, don't turn and fight.

★

Never test the depth of the water with both feet.

★

If you have something to say, raise your right hand and cover your mouth.

★

If at first you don't succeed... destroy all evidence that you tried.

★

Forgive and forget, but keep a list of names.

★

Don't kick a man when he's down... unless you're certain he won't get up.

★

When you go to court, remember your future is being decided by twelve people who weren't clever enough to get out of jury service.

★

Don't forget, friends help you move... real friends help you move bodies.

★

When all else fails... lower your standards.

★

Laugh in the face of danger... then run and hide until it goes away.

★

Don't be discouraged if you feel a failure... on some days even an erection can count as personal growth.

★

I've had a to-do list for as long as I can remember... But never finished it. It became a low self-esteem list.

★

Why do people say, "Get well soon?" Why don't they say, "Get well now"? Get well soon means, "Stay sick a bit longer".

It's the truth

If I had £2 for every time I'd played the National Lottery I'd have broken even.

★

I've got to lay off the alcohol. Doctor's orders. Well, I say "Doctor", I mean "Judge".

★

Life can be so strange, you know. It doesn't matter how quietly I strip naked and get in the bath, the birds always fly away and the park keeper always calls the police.

★

My Gran has been on cloud nine since the doctor told her yesterday that she has acute angina. That does it, like it or not she's having her hearing tested Monday.

★

If you only ever sleep with prostitutes does that make you buysexual?

★

Been to the gym for the first time this year. Gotta say didn't find it easy. Maybe I should get a satnav.

Oh yes, lockdown again

I got so desperate for things to do during the lockdown, I cut the grass on my front lawn once a week. And it was hard work. Well nail scissors do the job but I really must buy myself a mower.

★

Until this year I thought lockdown was a big lake in Scotland.

★

Just before lockdown was officially announced I went to the supermarket and filled two trolleys with groceries, household goods, toiletries, bottled water, beer and a half-dozen bottles of wine. The total cost was over £500. It was a lot of money, but I felt it was important to do it before all those idiots started panic-buying…

★

I spent the first four weeks of the lockdown in a hotel room. By the third week I was so bored, I sent down for another Bible.

★

I had to phone half-a-dozen taxi firms before I could find one willing to take me home and when he turned up I must say the driver was very considerate. He left the boot door open just wide enough to let me breathe.

★

My uncle took government advice to walk a couple of miles every day. Last we heard he was just outside Manchester.

★

After two months of self-isolation, I felt the walls of my house were closing in on me. Turns out I was just taking up more space because I'd put on two stone.

★

My cousin decided the lockdown would be the ideal time to grow a beard. Even though we all warned her it was a bad idea...

★

Self-isolation went on for so long, even hermits started to complain.

Light bulb moments

Q. How many train spotters does it take to change a light bulb?
A. Four. One to change it. One to hold his flask and Tupperware box of cheese-spread sandwiches. Another to hold the beige jumper his mother knitted for his 47th birthday. And one to make a note of the number of minutes it took the first one

to unscrew the old bulb and replace it with the new one. Because one day, it's possible that someone might want to know this information.

★

Q. Why does it take three accordion players to change a light bulb?

A. Because while the first one changes it, the second one has to wait next to the telephone in case the first one gets a last-minute offer of a paying gig. And it's the job of the third one to point out to the second one that he's wasting his time because none of them have ever had a paying gig, last-minute or otherwise.

★

Q. How many builders does it take to change a light bulb?

A. Well it all depends whether you want a patch-up job or something more permanent. It's entirely up to you, of course, but if this was my place I'd renew all the electrics; take that ceiling down and put up a brand new one; renew the damp course... and I'd seriously think about knocking that wall down and extending this room out into the garden to give twice the living space you've got now. Tell you what, as you seem like a nice couple, we won't charge you for the new bulb.

Q. How many Monty Python fans does it take to change a lightbulb?
A. Three. One to change it and two to recite the Dead Parrot sketch word-for-word.

★

Q. How many magicians does it take to change a light bulb?
A. Two. One to change it and one to misdirect you so you didn't see how the first one did it.

★

Q. How many anglers does it take to change a light bulb?
A. Two. One to change it and one to boast about the enormous size of the bulb he changed last year.

★

Q. How many Jeremy Corbyns does it take to change a lightbulb?
A. Who's Jeremy Corbyn?

★

Q. How many senior advisers to the Prime Minister does it take to change a light bulb?
A. Three. One to make a 600-mile round trip to get the bulb. One to change it. And one to drive a further 60 miles to a beauty spot because when the bulb was switched on it was so bright it hurt his eyes.

★

Q. How many hosts of *The One Show* does it take to change a light bulb?
A. All of them. But before they start, here's a tedious short film about the vanishing water voles of Lincolnshire.

★

Q. How many Cheryl Coles does it take to change a light bulb.

A. Two. One to do the actual changing and one to badly mime changing it.

★

Q. How many Welsh First Ministers does it take to change a light bulb?

A. I'm cautiously and carefully thinking about whether – at some point yet to be determined – I should put plans in place for a review to, hopefully, discuss the practicalities of creating a committee to formulate a strategy that will look forward to a time when we could implement a feasibility study that might, and I stress might, approach the possibility of changing the light bulb... although this is not set in stone.

★

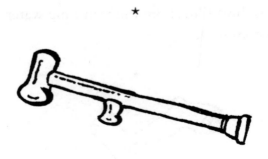

Q. How many telephone cold-callers does it take to change a light bulb?
A. This is beyond a joke. That's the fifth time today you've asked me that same question and my answer's just the same! I haven't had a recent motor accident that wasn't my fault!

★

Q. How many American Presidents does it take to change a light bulb?
A. That's a nasty question! Are you with CNN?

Medical mirth

A man goes to the doctor and says "Doctor. I'm suffering from terrible flatulence, constantly breaking wind wherever I go. Even outside in the waiting room. But fortunately it's odourless and silent. Can you do something about it? "

And the doctor says "I'm sure I can. But I'm more worried about the fact you've completely lost your sense of smell and your hearing!"

★

A man loses his ear in a terrible industrial accident and is taken to hospital. The surgeon tells him, "If you're willing, I'd like to try out a brand new surgical procedure that involves grafting a pig's ear, which is not dissimilar to a human ear, to the side of your head. Once it heals you should be able to hear just as well as you ever did."

The man agrees, the procedure is performed successfully and a couple of months later the patient returns for his follow-up appointment.

The surgeon examines the head, sits back in his chair and says, "Well, everything looks fine to me. Any problems, at all?"

And the man says, "As matter of fact there is one. I keep getting this crackling in my ear."

★

A man was in hospital awaiting a minor operation and was visited by the surgeon who was going to perform the procedure. The surgeon carefully explained what he'd be doing, told the patient not to worry and then asked, "Can you see that stunningly gorgeous willowy blonde nurse over there?"

The patient looked down the ward, saw the attractive nurse and said, "Yes. What about her?"

The doctor smiled and said, "I've been going out with her for two weeks!"

The patient was surprised. "Why are you telling me?"

"I'm telling everyone!" the doctor replied.

★

A man phones the maternity ward of his local hospital and says, "I'm enquiring about Mrs Wendy Jenkins who gave birth to a baby boy this morning".

The nurse says, "Mrs Jenkins is absolutely fine. Is this her first baby?"

And the man says "No. It's her husband!"

★

A man goes to the doctor and says "Doctor, you've got to help me. I think I must be a kleptomaniac. I can't stop going into shops and stealing things. Anything from designer clothes to electrical goods. Can you do something for me?".

The doctor said "Yes, I can write you out a prescription for a course of tablets. Take one a day for a month. If they don't work, come back and see me… and bring me an Armani suit and a wide-screen TV!"

★

A man sat in a doctor's waiting room, reciting the same thing to himself over and over "I really hope I'm ill. I really hope I'm ill!"

Finally, a fellow patient asked him why he kept repeating that and the man said, "Because I'd hate to be well and feel as bad as this!"

★

A man visits his doctor, complaining about a pain in his arm. The doctor asks, "Have you ever had this pain before?"

"Yes," says the man.

The doctor says, "Well you've got it again!"

★

A man rushes to his doctor and said "You've got to help me. I've got a £1 coin stuck in my left ear and a £2 coin stuck in my right ear!"

The doctor takes a look at him and says "How long have these coins been stuck in your ears?"

"Almost three years!" says the man.

The doctor is amazed and ask, "Why didn't you come and see me sooner?"

To which the man replies, "I didn't need the money until now!"

Funny that

While I was enjoying a latte in a coffee shop, I couldn't help notice three young girls sat together at a nearby table, all looking really sad. All of a sudden, one of them burst into tears and then the other two followed suit. I was so concerned I wandered over to their table, sat down and asked if there was anything I could do. They all shook their heads, blew their noses and stopped crying. To try and cheer them up, I ordered afternoon tea for all of us. When the waiter brought the teapot and cups I said, "Now who's going to be mother?" and they all started crying again....

★

I was watching a TV documentary about Bob Geldof the other day. It was fascinating. Apparently he pays a woman to come in twice a week to untidy his house.

★

See a pin and pick it up... and all day you'll have a pin!

Proverbs for the modern age

Too many cooks spoil the TV schedules.

★

A friend in need will soon be an ex-friend if you've got any sense.

★

As one door closes another one opens... if you haven't put that Ikea cabinet together properly.

★

Misery loves company. Why else would Adele sell so many CDs?

★

You can lead a horse to water but it's unlikely the manager of the swimming baths will allow him in.

★

You can't teach an old dog new tricks. So why not teach him some old ones?

★

Opportunity seldom knocks twice, so that was probably the Amazon delivery driver you just heard at your front door.

★

Beggars can't be choosers – although many of them do choose to sit near a cash machine.

★

The early bird catches the worm. And the tomcat that's been hanging around the garden all night catches the early bird.

★

Money is the root of all evil. Remind the vicar of that, next time he comes around with the collection plate.

★

Never look a gift horse in the mouth. And it's also good advice to stay well away from the other end… unless you're a vet.

★

Two heads are better than one. Although you might have trouble finding shirts to fit you.

★

All the world loves a lover. Unless he's run off with your wife.

★

Laugh and the world laughs with you. Keep laughing and eventually the world will phone for an ambulance.

★

You can't judge a book by its cover. So what's the point of having covers on books?

★

A fool and his money are soon parted. A very wise, amazingly generous African prince told me that in his e-mail offering to share £100,000 with me if I sent him £2,000 to pay his air fare to the UK.

★

Many a good tune is played on an old fiddle. But find a soundproof room before you try it.

Jokes by Dilwyn Phillips

A doctor held a stethoscope up to a Dai's chest.

Dai said, "Doc, how do I stand?

The doctor answered "That's what puzzles me!"

★

"But, your honour," said the man charged with dangerous driving. "The other guy was talking on his mobile and drinking a can of beer when I hit him."

"That's all very well," said the judge. "But he's entitled to do whatever he wants in his own conservatory."

★

A dog lover was just drifting off to sleep when she heard awful howling and moaning sounds. She rushed downstairs and found a dog locked together with a bitch who it seemed, had just come into heat.

She tried to separate them without success, and in desperation, called the local vet, who answered the phone in a very grumpy voice.

After she explained the problem to him, he advised her, "Hang up the phone and place it down alongside the dogs. I will then call you back and the noise of the ringing will make the male lose his erection and he will be able to withdraw."

"Do you think that will work?" she asked.

"Just worked for me," he replied.

★

"You'll be fine," the doctor said after finishing the young woman's surgery.

"But," she asked, "how long will it be before I am able to have a normal sex life again, doctor?"

The surgeon paused and a faraway look came into his eye.

The girl was alarmed. "What's the matter doctor? I will be all right, won't I?"

"Yes, you'll be fine," he said. "It's just that no-one has ever asked me that after having their tonsils out."

★

It's an age-old question: Is giving birth more painful than getting kicked in the nuts?

Well, look at it this way. A year or so after giving birth, a woman will often say, "It might be nice to have another child."

On the other hand, you never hear a guy say, "You know, I think it's time I had another kick in the nuts."

Great truths about growing old

1) Growing old is mandatory; growing up is optional.
2) Forget the health food. I need all the preservatives I can get.
3) You know you're old when you fall down – and wonder what else you can do while you're down there.
4) You're getting old when you get the same sensation from a rocking chair that you once got from a rollercoaster.
5) It's frustrating when you know all the answers but nobody bothers to ask you the questions.
6) Time may be a great healer, but it's a lousy beautician.
7) Wisdom comes with age, but sometimes age comes alone.

★

Helpful tips posted on a sign at a golf club in the Valleys
1. Back straight, knees bent
2. Feet shoulder width apart
3. Form a loose grip

4. Keep your head down
5. Stay out of the water
6. Try not to hit anyone
7. If you are taking too long, let others go ahead of you
8. Don't stand directly in front of others
9. Quiet please... while others are preparing
10. Don't take extra strokes

Well done. Now, flush the urinal, go outside, and tee off!

★

The Highways Agency recently examined more than 200 crows that had been found dead after being hit by vehicles on the approach to Brynglas tunnels at Newport. By analysing the paint residues on the birds it was found that 98 per cent had been killed by impact with lorries, while only 2 per cent were killed by cars.

An ornithological expert explained that when crows eat roadkill, they always have a look-out crow to warn of danger. While all the look-out crows could shout "Cah", not a single one could shout "Lorry".

★

Doctor to husband: "We have your wife here in hospital."

Husband: "How is she?"

Doctor: "I'm afraid she's critical."

Husband: "Ah, you get used to that."

★

I walked into the men's toilets with a glass of beer.

"Excuse me, mate, can you hold this while I have a wee?" I asked.

"No" he replied "But I'll hold your pint"

★

I had a leak in the roof over my dining room so I called a building contractor to take a look at it.

"When did you first notice the leak?" he asked.

I told him, "Last night, when it took me two hours to finish my soup!"

★

Mr Evans went to see his GP and told him, "Doctor, my wife is pregnant but we always used protection and the condom never broke, so how is this possible?"

"I will tell you a story," the doctor said. "There once was a hunter who always used a gun but one day he took his umbrella by mistake. When a lion jumped out in front of him he used his umbrella just like his gun and shot the lion dead."

Mr Evans laughed out loud. "Nonsense! someone else must have shot that lion."

The doctor smiled. "Good, you understood the story – next patient please."

Actual entries on hospital charts (part one)

1. She has no rigours or shaking chills, but her husband states she was very hot in bed last night.
2. Patient has chest pain if she lies on her left side for over a year.
3. On the second day the knee was better, and on the third day it disappeared.
4. The patient is tearful and crying constantly. She also appears to be depressed.

5. The patient has been depressed since she began seeing me in 1993.
6. Discharge status: Alive, but without my permission.
7. Healthy appearing decrepit 69-year-old male, mentally alert but forgetful.

★

Superman could have become a doctor, using his X-ray vision to detect life-threatening tumours. But no, we really needed another journalist.

★

My dad always said, "The first rule of theatre is to always leave them wanting more."

Great bloke.

Terrible anaesthetist.

★

A couple is lying in bed. The man says, "I am going to make you the happiest woman in the world..."

The woman replies, "I'll miss you…"

★

Little Bobby and Jenny are only ten years old, but they know they are in love.

One day they decide they want to get married, so Bobby goes to Jenny's father to ask him for her hand.

Bobby bravely walks up to him and says, "Mr Smith, me and Jenny are in love and I want to ask you for her hand in marriage."

Thinking that this is simply adorable, Mr Smith replies, "Well, Bobby, you are only 10. Where will you two live?"

Without even taking a moment to think about it, Bobby replies, "In Jenny's room. It's bigger than mine and we can both fit there nicely."

Mr Smith says with a huge grin, "Okay, then how will you live? You're not old enough to get a job. You'll need to support Jenny."

Again, Bobby instantly replies, "Our allowance. Jenny gets five quid a week and I make six quid a week. That's about 44 quid-plus a month, so that should do us just fine."

Mr Smith is impressed Bobby has put so much thought into this.

"Well, Bobby, it seems like you have everything figured out. I just have one more question. What will you do if the two of you should have little children of your own?"

Bobby just shrugs his shoulders and says, "Well, we've been lucky so far."

Actual entries on hospital charts (part two)

1. The patient refused autopsy.
2. The patient has no previous history of suicides.
3. Patient has left white blood cells at another hospital.
4. Patient's medical history has been remarkably insignificant with only a 40lb weight gain in the last three days.
5. Patient had waffles for breakfast and anorexia for lunch.
6. She is numb from her toes down.
7. While in ER, she was examined, X-rated and sent home.

★

Brenda and Steve took their six-year-old son to the doctor. With some hesitation, they explained that although their little angel appeared to be in good health, they were concerned about his rather small penis.

After examining the child, the doctor confidently declared, "Just feed him pancakes. That should solve the problem."

The next morning when the boy arrived at breakfast, there was a large stack of warm pancakes in the middle of the table.

"Gee, Mam," he exclaimed, "for me?"

"Just take two," Brenda replied. "The rest are for your father"

★

Ianto, a 70-year-old, extremely wealthy widower, shows up at the Country Club with a breathtakingly beautiful and very sexy blonde who hangs over Ianto's arm and listens intently to his every word.

His buddies at the club are amazed. At their very first chance, they corner him and ask, "Ianto, how'd you get the trophy girlfriend?"

Ianto replies, "Girlfriend? She's my wife!"

They're knocked over: "So, how'd you persuade her to marry you?"

"I lied about my age," Ianto replied.

"What? Did you tell her you were only 50?"

Ianto smiled, "No, I told her I was 90."

★

A young doctor moved to a small Valleys rural community to replace a doctor who was retiring. The older doctor suggested he accompany him on his rounds to introduce him to his patients.

At the first house, the woman complained, "I've had stomach trouble and been sick a few times."

The older doctor said, "Well, you've probably been overdoing the fresh fruit. Cut back on the amount you've been eating and see if that does the trick."

As they left, the younger man was amazed. "You didn't even examine that woman?" he said. How did you come to the diagnosis so quickly?"

"I didn't have to. Did you notice that I dropped my stethoscope on the floor in there? When I bent over to pick it up I noticed half-a-dozen banana peels in the waste bin. That was probably what was making her sick."

The younger doctor said "That's very clever. I think I'll try that next time."

Arriving at the next house, they spent several minutes talking with a younger woman. She reported that she just didn't have the energy she once did and said, "I'm feeling terribly run down lately."

"You've probably been doing too much for the church," the younger doctor told her. "Perhaps you should cut back a bit and see if that helps."

As they left, the elder doctor said, "I know that woman well and your diagnosis is most certainly correct as she's very active in the local church, but how did you arrive at it?"

"I did what you did at the last house. I dropped my stethoscope and, when I bent down to retrieve it, I noticed the vicar under the bed."

★

Ken feared his wife Jude wasn't hearing as well as she used to and he thought she might need a hearing aid.

Not quite sure how to approach her he called the family doctor to discuss the problem.

The doctor told him there was a simple test he could perform.

"Here's what you do," said the doctor. "Stand about 40 feet away from her and in a normal conversational speaking tone see if she hears you. If not go to 30 feet, then 20 feet and so on until you get a response."

That evening his wife was in the kitchen cooking dinner and he was in the den – about 40 feet away. In a normal tone he asked, "Honey, what's for dinner?"

No response.

So Ken moved closer to the kitchen, about 30 feet from his wife and repeated, "Jude, what's for dinner?"

Still no response.

Next he moved into the dining room where he was about 20 feet from his wife and asked, "Honey, what's for dinner?"

Again he got no response.

So he walked up to the kitchen door, about 10 feet away. "Honey, what's for dinner?"

Again – no response.

So he walked right up behind her, tapped her on the shoulder and said. "Jude, what's for dinner?"

"For heaven's sake, Ken, for the FIFTH time, CHICKEN!"

★

I was always taught to respect my elders, but it keeps getting harder to find one.

Actual entries on hospital charts (part three)

1. The skin was moist and dry.
2. Occasional constant infrequent headaches.
3. Rectal examination revealed a normal-size thyroid.
4. She stated that she had been constipated for most of her life until she got a divorce.
5. I saw your patient today, who is still under our car for physical therapy.

6. Both breasts are equal and reactive to light and accommodation.
7. Examination of genitalia reveals that he is circus sized.

★

Learn from your parents' mistakes – use birth control!

★

A farmer from Mid Wales stopped at a local restaurant following a day of roaming around in Benidorm.

While sipping his wine, he noticed a sizzling, scrumptious-looking platter being served at the next table. Not only did it look good, the smell was wonderful.

He asked the waiter, "What is that you just served – it looks and smells great."

The waiter replied, "*Sí señor*, you have excellent taste! Those are called *cojones de toro*, testicles from the bull fight this morning. A great delicacy!"

The farmer said, "What the hell, bring me an order."

The waiter replied, "I am so sorry, *señor*. There is only one serving per day because there is only one bull fight each morning. If you come early and place your order, we will be sure to save you this delicacy."

The next morning, the farmer returned early, placed his order, and that evening was served the one and only special delicacy of the day.

After a few bites, inspecting his platter, he called to the waiter and said, "These are delicious, but they are much, much smaller than the ones I saw you serve yesterday."

The waiter shrugged his shoulders and replied, "*Sí señor*. Sometimes the bull, he do not lose."

★

Father Norton woke up one Sunday morning and, realising it was an exceptionally beautiful and sunny early spring day, decided he just had to play golf. So he told the associate pastor that he was feeling sick and persuaded him to say mass for him that day.

As soon as the associate pastor left the room, Father Norton headed out of town to a golf course about 40 miles away. This way he knew he wouldn't accidentally meet anyone he knew from his parish.

Setting up on the first tee, he was alone. After all, it was Sunday morning and everyone else was in church!

Looking down from the heavens, St Peter leaned over to the Lord and exclaimed, "You're not going to let him get away with this, are you?"

The Lord sighed, and said, "No, I guess not."

Just then Father Norton hit a beautiful shot straight towards the pin. It dropped just short of it, rolled a few feet and plopped into the hole. A 420-yard hole in one!

St Peter was astonished. He looked at the Lord and asked, "Why did you let him do that?"

The Lord smiled and replied, "Who's he going to tell?"

★

A priest was being honoured at his retirement dinner after 25 years in the parish. The guest of honour, who was due to make the presentation and give a speech was delayed, so the priest decided to say his own few words while they waited.

"I got my first impression of the parish from the first confession I heard here," he recalled. "I thought I had been assigned to a terrible place. The very first person who entered my confessional told me he had stolen a television set and, when questioned by the police, was able to lie his way out of it. He had stolen money from his parents; embezzled from his employer; had an affair with his boss's wife; had sex with his boss's 17-year old daughter on numerous occasions; taken illegal drugs; had several extra-marital affairs; was arrested several times for public nudity and gave an STD to his sister-in-law.

"I was appalled that one person could do so many awful things. But as the days went on, I learned that my people were not all like that and I had, indeed, come to a fine parish full of good and loving people."

Just as the priest finished his talk, the guest of honour arrived, a local MP and prominent member of the congregation. He apologised profusely for his late arrival and began his talk.

"I'll never forget the first day our parish priest arrived," said the MP. "In fact, I had the honour of being the first person ever to go to him for confession."

Actual entries on hospital charts (part four)

1. The lab test indicated abnormal lover function.
2. The patient was to have a bowel resection. However, he took a job as a stockbroker instead.
3. Skin: somewhat pale, but present.
4. The pelvic exam will be done later on the floor.
5. Patient was seen in consultation by Dr Blank, who felt we should sit on the abdomen, and I agree.
6. Large brown stool ambulating in the hall.
7. Patient has two teenage children but no other abnormalities.

★

A father walks into a restaurant with his young son. He gives the young boy three 5p pieces to play with to keep him occupied. Suddenly the boy starts choking and turns blue in the face.

The father realises the boy has swallowed the coins and starts slapping him on the back. The boy coughs up two of the coins, but keeps choking.

A well-dressed, serious-looking woman, in a blue business suit is sitting at the coffee bar reading a newspaper and sipping a cup of coffee. At the sound of the commotion, she looks up, puts her coffee cup down, folds the newspaper and places it on the counter, gets up from her seat and makes her way, unhurriedly, across the restaurant.

Reaching the boy, the woman carefully pulls down his pants; takes hold of the boy's testicles and begins to squeeze and twist, gently at first and then ever so firmly. After a few seconds the boy convulses violently and coughs up the last coin, which the woman deftly catches in her free hand.

Releasing the boy's testicles, the woman hands the coin to the father and walks back to her seat in the coffee bar without saying a word.

As soon as he is sure his son has suffered no ill-effects, the father rushes over to the woman and thanks her profusely saying, "I've never seen anybody do anything like that before, it was fantastic! Are you a doctor?"

"No," the woman says. "A divorce lawyer."

★

When I was young I decided I wanted to be a doctor, so I took the entrance exam to go to medical school.

One of the questions was to rearrange the letters P-N-E-I-S into a word describing an important human body part which is most useful when erect. Those who answered 'spine' are doctors today.

★

When people say, "It's always the last place you look" – of course it is. Why the hell would you keep looking after you've found it?

★

Doctor to a pregnant prostitute, "Do you know who the father is?"

She rolls her eyes: "Hey, if you ate a can of beans would you know which one made you fart?"

★

A little boy got lost at the YMCA and found himself in the women's locker room. When he was spotted, the room burst into shrieks, with ladies grabbing towels and running for cover.

The little boy watched in amazement and then asked, "What's the matter, haven't you ever seen a little boy before?"

★

It was the end of the day when I parked my police van in front of the station. As I gathered my equipment, my canine partner, Jake, was barking, and I saw a little boy staring in at me.

"Is that a dog you got back there?" he asked.

"It sure is," I replied.

Puzzled, the boy looked at me and then towards the back of the van. Finally he said, "What'd he do?"

★

Towards the end of the Sunday service, the minister asked, "How many of you have forgiven your enemies?" Four-fifths of the congregation held up their hands.

The minister then repeated his question. All responded this time, except one elderly man.

"Mr Williams," said the minister. "Are you not willing to forgive your enemies?"

"I don't have any," he replied gruffly.

"Mr Williams, that is very unusual. How old are you?"

"Ninety-eight," he replied. The congregation stood up and clapped their hands.

"Oh, Mr Williams, would you please come down to the front and tell us all how a person can live 98 years and not have an enemy in the world?"

The old man tottered down the aisle, stopped in front of the pulpit, turned around, faced the congregation, and said simply, "I outlived the bastards."